CW01508262

THE GREAT BOOK OF ANIMAL KNOWLEDGE

# THE HIPPO

Gigantic Creature of the African Rivers

All Rights Reserved. All written content in this book may NOT
be reproduced in any form or by any means, including scanning,
photocopying, or otherwise without prior written permission of the
copyright holder. Copyright © 2014

Some Rights Reserved. All photographs contained in this book
are under the Creative Commons license and can be copied and
redistributed in any medium or format for any purpose, even
commercially. However, you must give appropriate credit, provide a
link to the license, and indicate if changes were made.

# Introduction

Photo by Stig Nygaard (flickr.com/stignygaard) via: freeforcommercialuse.org

The hippopotamus or hippo is a large plant eating mammal found in Africa. The name hippopotamus means 'river horse'. Hippos are the heaviest surviving even-toed animals. Hippos are recognized by their barrel-shaped body and their big mouth and teeth.

# What Hippos Look Like

Photo by Matt Biddulph (flickr.com/mbiddulph) via: freeforcommercialuse.org

Hippos are usually colored grey or dark brown. They have a huge head with small eyes and ears. They also have short legs and hairless bodies. Hippos may look chubby and slow but they can easily outrun a human. So make sure you keep your distance from an aggressive hippo.

# Size and Weight

Photo by I Love Trees (flickr.com/ilovetrees) via: freeforcommercialuse.org

The average adult hippo weights up to 1,500 kg (3,300 pounds). That's about the same weight as an average car! Baby hippos weigh between 25 to 50 kg (55 and 110 pounds) and will grow up to 4.5 feet tall.

# Teeth

Photo by Olivier B. (flickr.com/olivierbardin) via: freeforcommercialuse.org

Adult hippos have thirty six teeth. Their largest teeth are called tusks and it's used for fighting and inflicting wounds on their enemies. They use their flat molars at the back of their mouth to chew up vegetation.

# Hippo Sweat

Photo by Tambako The Jaguar (flickr.com/tambako) via: freeforcommercialuse.org

When a hippo becomes too dry, its skin secretes a red fluid. Before, people thought that the red fluid was blood and that hippos sweat blood. Now we know that it isn't blood but a skin moisturizer that helps protect their body from the sun and bacteria.

# Where The Hippo Lives

Photo by khym54 (flickr.com/khym54) via: freeforcommercialuse.org

Hippos inhabit rivers, lakes and swamps. Hippos love water. When the weather gets hot, they keep themselves cool by staying in the water or mud.

# Where The Hippo Sleeps

Photo by Farhan Chawla (flickr.com/farhan) via: freeforcommercialuse.org

Hippos sleep underwater and when they need to breathe, they float to the top. Hippos can hold their breath for 6 minutes at a time. Do you think you can hold your breath that long?

# What The Hippo Eats

Photo by Xiaojun Deng (flickr.com/hktang) via: freeforcommercialuse.org

After a hot day cools, the hippo will go out of the water to find food. Hippos are grazers just like cows, which means they eat green plants and grass.

# Hungry Hippo

Photo by Chris Eason (flickr.com/mister-e) via: freeforcommercialuse.org

Hippos can eat grass for six straight hours! However, they only consume about 80 pounds, which is very little compared to their huge size. Hippos are lazy animals so they don't need much food for energy.

# Drinking

Photo by Marieke IJsendoorn-Kuijpers (flickr.com/mape_s) via: freeforcommercialuse.org

Hippos can drink up to 56 gallons of water in just one day! They also get some water from the grass they eat, but that's not enough water for them. This is why they are never far away from places with lots of water.

# Swimming

Photo by Pete (flickr.com/comedynose) via: freeforcommercialuse.org

Hippos are very good swimmers. They swim by kicking their strong back legs. When they go under the water, their eyes, nostrils and ears all close up so water doesn't get in.

# Aggression

Photo by Nils Rinaldi (flickr.com/nilsrinaldi) via: freeforcommercialuse.org

Hippos are the most aggressive animals in the world. Male hippos can be quite dangerous when their home is threatened. Even other dangerous animals like crocodiles won't mess with them. Mother hippos are very protective of their young and they will attack anything that tries to harm their little one.

# Social Life

Photo by Brian Harries (flickr.com/129936023@N02) via: freeforcommercialuse.org

Hippos are social animals and live in groups called pods or schools. These groups can range from 5 individual hippos to more than 30. Often, there is a male leader who watches over all the other hippos.

# Noisy Hippos

Photo by Stig Nygaard (flickr.com/stignygaard) via: freeforcommercialuse.org

Hippos are very loud animals. They can make snorting sounds as loud as the speakers at a rock concert! They can also make other sounds like grumbling and wheezing.

# Breeding

Photo by Alias 0591 (flickr.com/renemensen) via: freeforcommercialuse.org

Hippos look very similar so it's hard to tell whether it's a male or female. Female hippos are ready to breed at 6 years of age and males are ready when they're 7 years old. The breeding takes place at the beginning of the wet season. A mother can only give birth to one hippo. But sometimes, she can also give birth to twins.

# Baby Hippo

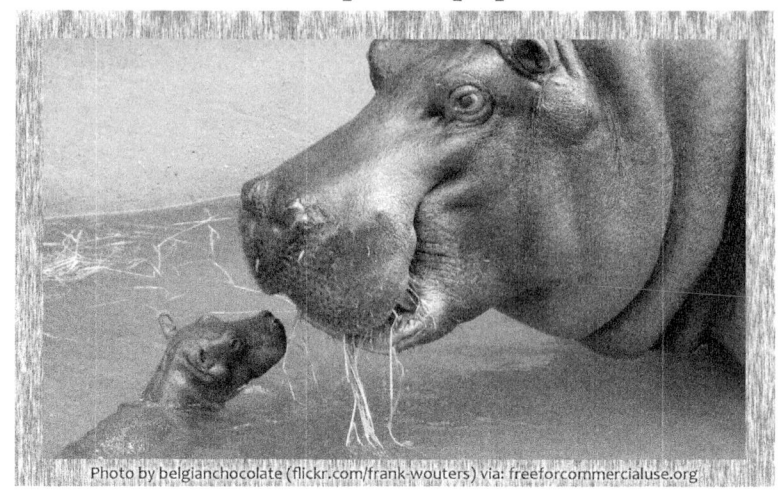

Photo by belgianchocolate (flickr.com/frank-wouters) via: freeforcommercialuse.org

Baby Hippos are born underwater. A baby hippo, also called calf, will drink its mother's milk when she's on land or swim underwater to suckle. They also sometimes climb on their mother back to rest. Baby hippos stop drinking their mother's milk at about 5 to 7 years old.

# The Life of a Hippo

Photo by Steve Slater (flickr.com/wildlife_encounters) via: freeforcommercialuse.org

Hippos leave the water at night and travel on land to eat grass and other plants. When a hippo is threatened by another animal, they run for the water. Hippos usually live up to 40 – 50 years.

# Predators

Photo by Paul Williams (flickr.com/bluelemur) via: freeforcommercialuse.org

Hippos don't have many natural predators because of their huge size, strong mouth and sharp teeth. Their only real concern is the crocodile and lion. In the water, crocodiles hunt baby hippos when they are far from their mothers. On land, lions and hyenas are the biggest problem for young hippos or sick hippos.

# Hippo Defense

Photo by ijyt (flickr.com/ijyt) via: freeforcommercialuse.org

Hippos look like peaceful animals when they're resting in the water. However, hippos are very fierce animals and they can crush anyone who gets close to their territory. Some male hippos will even kill baby hippos in defense of their home.

# Large Hippo

Photo by Gusjer (flickr.com/gusjer) via: freeforcommercialuse.org

There are two kinds of hippos. The large hippo and the pygmy hippo. Large hippos are the most common hippos. When you think of a hippo, you're probably thinking of the large hippo. Large hippos like to live with a lot of other hippos.

# Pygmy Hippo

Photo by Eric Kilby (flickr.com/ekilby) via: freeforcommercialuse.org

A pygmy hippos is a smaller version of the large hippo. Pygmy hippos spend more time on land than on water. They have longer legs to help them run through the forests. Because pygmy hippos don't always stay in water, they don't need elevated eyes and nostrils.

# Get the next book in this series!

## THE RHINO: Horned Beast of the African Grasslands

(Log on to Facebook.com/GazelleCB for more info)

For more information about our books, discounts and updates, please Like us on Facebook!

Facebook.com/GazelleCB

Printed in Great Britain
by Amazon

73308213R00020